Amidst the Flurry

A collection of poetry by Noor Zohdy

For all the people who helped me see all the magic amidst the flurry.

Those who have helped me marvel,
And not walk by nature's wonders in a hurry.

Those who have made me stop and look above,
As the sky to the morning bends.

Those who have made me see, that in that moment,
All at once, magic descends.

The theme of this collection of poetry stems from its first poem. One of my very favourite set of lines I've ever written is:

For, in that curious silence,
One can frankly see,

A little leaf standing in adamance,
As if to call,
"Oh, do care to look at me!"

This sentiment is truly something I have hoped to weave throughout the entirety of this collection. Poetry has this curious revitalising sense about it, where you can look at something incredibly commonplace, and it is as if your senses are heightened, and everything around you steps forward in its overwhelming beauty and breathtaking fascination. Take Wordsworth, for instance, is there not something more magical in a daffodil, once you hear of how they "toss their heads in sprightly dance"? When John Keats said, "Poetry...should strike the reader as a wording of his own highest thoughts, and appear almost a remembrance," he described this perennial telescope poetry leaves upon us; we suddenly see that stars twinkle just so. It is a tremendous medium of discovery: and as poetry expands our hearts to be able to perceive these wonders around us, it also gives us leave to forever explore these otherwise unseen gardens of vibrance.

Amidst the Flurry

A swirl of snow
Laughs in merry fervour,
To the expectant bough,
Enchanting the observer.

A lace of hush,
Utmost grace as fell,
Quick to rise a blush,
Winter cast her spell.

To muse upon sight,
A nature of repose,
Is falsity resound,
To deem such flight.

As the artist shall agree,

It cloaks the very same,

To be true it's but this time,

Glittered with delight.

Can one not love such scenery,

So without blight!

The happy surroundings,

Frosted all in white.

Yet, to be found in such quiet,

An eye may just find,

All but the most,

Intricately designed.

For, in that curious silence,

One can frankly see,

A little leaf standing in adamance,

As if to call,

"Oh, do care to look at me!"

Plus tôt

A ripple comes in sight,

We upon it dart,

Can it be the right?

Must we heave the heart?

It trickles below,

How we chase each drop,

For where may it flow—

For when shall it stop?

The curious glide,

Is cause of such alarm,

For in the former trees reside,

A heart's haven from harm.

But trees it shall flee,

Beyond them it passes,

But sombre it shan't be,

However foreign the masses.

Untouched by plight,

It is merely change's bright ray,

As embark of flight,

Is no cause of dismay.

For beyond the bough,

Of cherished and certain,

Lies all we may know,

Just beyond the curtain.

To See the Morning Rain

To the welcoming of dawn,
A pattering cascade in delicate ribbons of
grace,
Smiles upon presiding angst,
Tinting the below an enamouring hidden
lace.

The heavy falter lifted,
Quiet and serene,
A dear greeting gifted,
A respite sure to glean.

A smile becomes of those who peer yonder,
A clamber voices not of ponder,

But excitable conventional glee,
'Why, such weather there may be!'

But upon such silence within,
A smile chances a whisper of humble
wonder,
Among the soden and glistening street,
Becomes the question,
Who else may this morning rain meet?

Dear Lovely Garden

Dear lovely garden,
Thank you dearly, for such wonderful cheer,
All you have taught, twinkled and
brightened,
As a blue brook shines and glitters clear.

When a bird peers down from a nearby
branch,
And looks at the ripples of such wonder,
As they pan out and flow in merry dance,
The bird flutters from the tree to discover
All the kindness in each current flowing,
As its heart fills with gratitude and its eyes
smile upon a lily, glowing.

Night Sky

Frost dances through the air, as I step upon
the ice, glossy as a dream.
Before me a wink and twinkle of the
ground offers a familiar gleam.
Knowing seems the ground, as the sky
overhead appears a hasty veil,
For I know the day has ceased, yet how can
such bleakness prevail?
I feel a glide, but hardly walk, as the dim
light shines upon a raven ahead.
I daresay I quite alarmed the inky bird,
how eager was my hurried tread.
I hasten for I must know,
What caused the nighttime unrest as so?

With a flutter of ethereal wings, I stare as
they lift away,
I stare as I embark along the truest
nighttime sleigh.
Through the dismal dark curtain I see the
wings aim at swift,
Vibrance of all colours I saw, the stars
smile, indeed, a truest gift.
I looked about in such excitement, where
had the dim gone?
I saw the true beauty of night, I dreaded
the intruding dawn.

Owl-light

In the twilight hours,
Where owl-light resides,
It is the darkness that towers,
The light that ebbs in tides.

The stars hang ahead,
By the strength of the moon,
They dangle by mere thread,
Descend down they shall soon.

They unfurl their wings,
And hoot through flight,
They look to the springs,
Blessed beauty by moonlight.

The hero of the land,

Takes his grand white wings,

Upon flight to the grand,

Branch for night's kings.

Along the phantom cliffs,

Swept by quiet sea waves,

Along the hero gifts,

Goes greeting the caves.

The dove of the night,

Hoots a song of hope,

Weaving the faltering light,

With her silver-spinning rope.

The spotted owl descends,

With his solemn decree,
"Where the fern shall meet ends,
So shall the lives soon flee."

They weave their mark,
Spell of mysterious and true,
Until the voice of the lark,
Reminds them adieu.

The flood of the sea,
Echoes its deep howl,
As the sweeping dawn,
Hastens the final owl.

October

Winter frost,
An autumnal air,
One seems lost,
Such wonder is there.

Season's Lace

The little snowflake takes mount,

As a quiet and white winter falls.

The thistledown prances about,

As spring graces earth's walls.

How the two never meet,

Face to face,

Is such a curious feat,

Both their very own lace.

Signs from the sky

The dappled sunlight,

The cascading snow,

The rain in quick flight,

The world shines aglow.

From the light of day,

As the robin takes flight,

The dusk soon make way,

For the enchantment of night.

The thistledown follows,

It climbs the sky,

Morning welcomes the swallows,

As they laugh on by.

The flame of the sky,
Soon falls to the moon,
By its light the owls fly,
Weaving a nightly tune.

The stars, true pearls,
Cast glitter to life below,
The bat's wing unfurls,
In its eye, the subtle glow.

Soon the sun is unveiled,
It shines with undying rays,
And clouds have prevailed,
Over the night's starry blaze.

In God we trust,

In each day that arrives,

For the sky glimmers a gold dust,

Over each of our lives.

Sunset Colours

I reside where the sun trickles beyond the
horizon,
I am painted from the strokes of the
departing day.
I am left to linger among the silence,
When most glances are too surely turned
away.

I glide to and fro, for the sun deserves a
good show after such light,
I smile and leave my final gleam,
Before the oncoming of the glimmering
night.

To a dancing friendship from a singing
heart

High above the stars are singing,
Their song and laughter fill the sky,
And on this day their music's bringing
Love by birds, who flutter by.

For down below, there is a soul,
Two, that hold each other close,
Their hearts together forever whole,
Dancing through the highs and lows.

They leap and frolic through the lake,
They smile and glitter through the storm,
Such happy song will always make

Two midnight stars in human form.

Wings Through Mist

As night sweeps its curtain by,

Tucked away the stars still glimmer,

As the sun boldly paints the sky,

Its spirited, bright, and dappled shimmer.

Perched upon a star,

I look down with wist,

How it seems so very far,

A path twined with mist.

But as I peer down below,

I see my kind all in flutter,

Fly with bliss like merry snow,

Then, amid their dance, I utter,

"Why may I not leap?
And descend with all such flurry?
Is it this star that seems to keep
me in such hopeless, fitful worry?"

For beyond this star I see,
A new home, broad and fair,
One that beckons me to flee,
And soar high through the air.

I feel mist fall to pearl,
One like never before,
As my wings finally unfurl,
I am now free to explore.

From my heart to yours

From my heart to yours,
Remember the sky,
The love that it pours,
As a bird flutters by.

Nature and the sky of blue,
The birds and fluffy clouds,
With their whole heart dearly love you,
And sing for you aloud.

May your heart be full,
Of love and song,
May it cloak you like warm wool,
May it keep your heart forever strong,

Love always at hand, a pocketful.

A Daisy's Prance

There! The radiant daisy,
With its glowing petals,
Its magical shine.

There! The thistledown flies,
And so quickly it settles,
Like the heart jumps to joy,
When it once again meets
 A friend's eyes.

Thistledown Flight

The thistledown flies,
It mounts the sky,
I feel my heart rise,
As they flutter by.

I find a keen feeling of hope,
A bright sense of light,
As their silver-spinning rope,
Takes me aboard in flight.

Up high above

Up high above,
There, atop the sky,
Flies the merriment and love
Of a new friendship by.

Each cloud and bird
Looks and smiles,
At the beauty of our world,
As it transcends miles and miles.

It is as the robin takes off

It is the robin takes off,
Dancing through flight,
Like a midnight star help high aloft,
That twinkles, so forever bright.

It is as the leap of a fawn,
Upon autumnal leaves,
As the smile of the dawn,
Weaves eternal love wreaths.

.

Bright and radiant as the rainbow,

Gentle as the sky that laughs above,

May your days beckon so much glow,

May they be filled to the brim with laughter

and love.

As the sunshine casts light upon the day,

Here, a piece of my heart I lend,

May it fall upon yours an undying ray,

Happily from Noor, your affectionate friend.

Made in the USA
Middletown, DE
26 June 2021